DK findout!
Solar System

Author and consultant: Sarah Cruddas

Project editor Sam Priddy
Senior designer Katie Knutton
Designers Emma Hobson, Lucy Sims
Editorial assistant Kathleen Teece
Managing editor Laura Gilbert
Managing art editor Diane Peyton Jones
Picture researcher Surya Sarangi
Pre-production producer Dragana Puvacic
Producer Srijana Gurung
Art director Martin Wilson
Publisher Sarah Larter
Publishing director Sophie Mitchell

Educational consultant Jacqueline Harris

First published in Great Britain in 2016
This paperback edition first published in 2017 by
Dorling Kindersley Limited
80 Strand, London, WC2R 0RL

Copyright © 2016, 2017 Dorling Kindersley Limited
A Penguin Random House Company
10 9 8 7 6 5 4 3 2 1
001–309511–Oct/2017

A CIP catalogue record for this book
is available from the British Library.
ISBN: 978-0-2413-3130-9

Printed and bound in China

A WORLD OF IDEAS:
SEE ALL THERE IS TO KNOW

www.dk.com

Contents

The Moon

The Earth

Saturn

Pluto

Asteroid

The Sun

Jupiter

Space probe

Astronaut

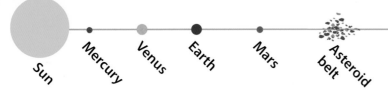

Sun Mercury Venus Earth Mars Asteroid belt Jupiter Saturn

What is the Solar System?

The Solar System is made up of our star, called the Sun, and everything that travels, or orbits, around it. This includes eight planets and their moons, dwarf planets, asteroids, comets, and smaller bits of rock and dust. The Solar System is one of many solar systems that exist in the Universe.

Asteroids

Asteroids are lumps of rock and metal left over from when the Solar System first formed. Most can be found in the asteroid belt, which is located between the planets Mars and Jupiter.

Comets

Comets are cosmic snowballs of rock, ice, and dust. When one passes near to the Sun, it heats up and forms a tail.

Gas planets

The four outer planets – Jupiter, Saturn, Uranus, and Neptune – are the largest planets in the Solar System. They are mostly made of gas and spacecraft are unable to land on them.

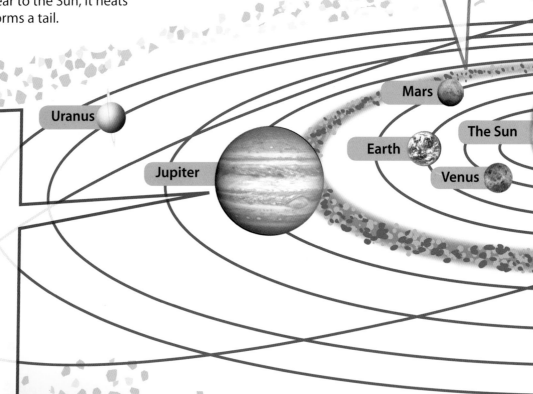

Uranus

Jupiter

Mars

Earth

The Sun

Venus

Uranus

Neptune

Pluto

Kuiper Belt

Rocky planets

Closest to the Sun are the four rocky planets – Mercury, Venus, Earth, and Mars. They all began their existence in the same way, but over time became very different worlds.

Super-sized

The Solar System is so big that if the Sun were the size of a basketball, the Earth would be the size of a sesame seed – and it would be located more than 25 m (80 ft) away!

The Kuiper Belt
This ring of icy rocks lies beyond the path that Neptune follows around the Sun.

Dwarf planets

Dwarf planets, such as Pluto, also travel around the Sun. These worlds are smaller than the other planets. Scientists think there may be dozens of undiscovered dwarf planets hiding in the Solar System.

Pluto

Mercury

Asteroid belt

Neptune

Saturn

! WOW!

Scientists believe the **Solar System** began to form around **4.6 billion** years ago.

The Milky Way

The Solar System is located in the Milky Way, a huge spiral galaxy containing billions of stars. They are grouped in "arms" that spiral outwards. All of the stars are travelling around a point at the centre. Scientists think there is a supermassive black hole located there that sucks in anything that gets too close to it.

The night sky

On a clear, dark night it is possible to see the Milky Way stretching across the sky as a bright, cloudy band. Although the Milky Way is a spiral galaxy, it doesn't look like it from Earth because we are inside it!

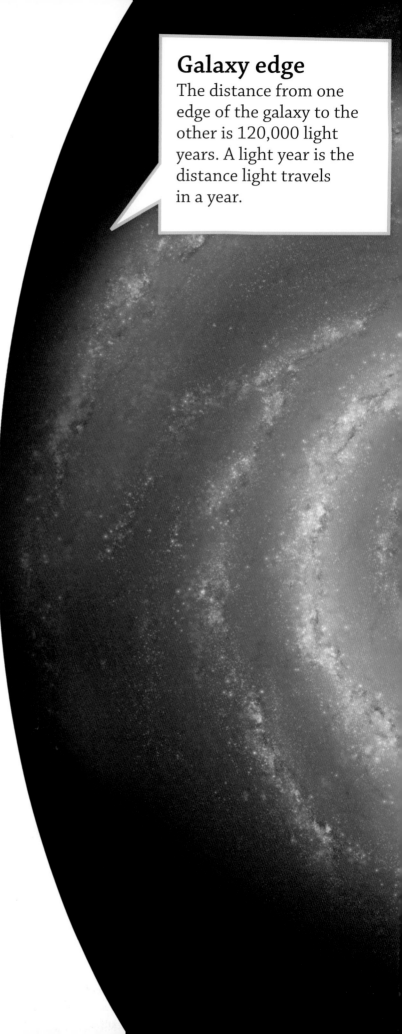

Galaxy edge

The distance from one edge of the galaxy to the other is 120,000 light years. A light year is the distance light travels in a year.

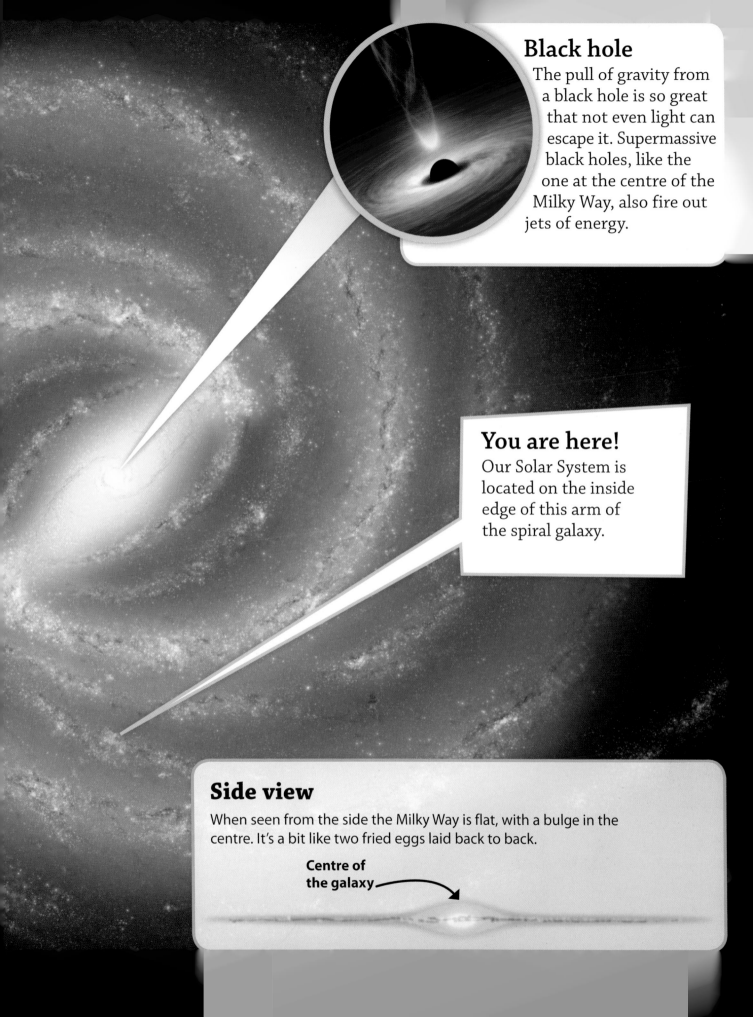

Black hole

The pull of gravity from a black hole is so great that not even light can escape it. Supermassive black holes, like the one at the centre of the Milky Way, also fire out jets of energy.

You are here!

Our Solar System is located on the inside edge of this arm of the spiral galaxy.

Side view

When seen from the side the Milky Way is flat, with a bulge in the centre. It's a bit like two fried eggs laid back to back.

Centre of
the galaxy

The Sun

Located at the centre of the Solar System is the Sun. It is a star, like the ones you see in the night sky. A burning ball of gas, made of mostly hydrogen and helium, it provides us with the heat we need to survive. The Sun is so massive that its gravity – the force that pulls things together – keeps the planets in orbit around it.

Solar flare

Huge eruptions from the surface of the Sun are called solar prominences. They form loops because of the Sun's invisible magnetic field.

FACT FILE

» **Name:** Sun

» **Surface temperature:** 5,500°C (9,930°F)

» **Core temperature:** 15 million°C (27 million°F)

» **Width:** 1,392,684 km (865,374 miles)

Our star

Energy is constantly being generated deep within the Sun. It can take up to 100,000 years for energy to reach the surface, but then it only takes 8 minutes to reach the Earth!

How big is the Sun?

The Sun is so ginormous that all of the planets of the Solar System could fit inside it hundreds of times over.

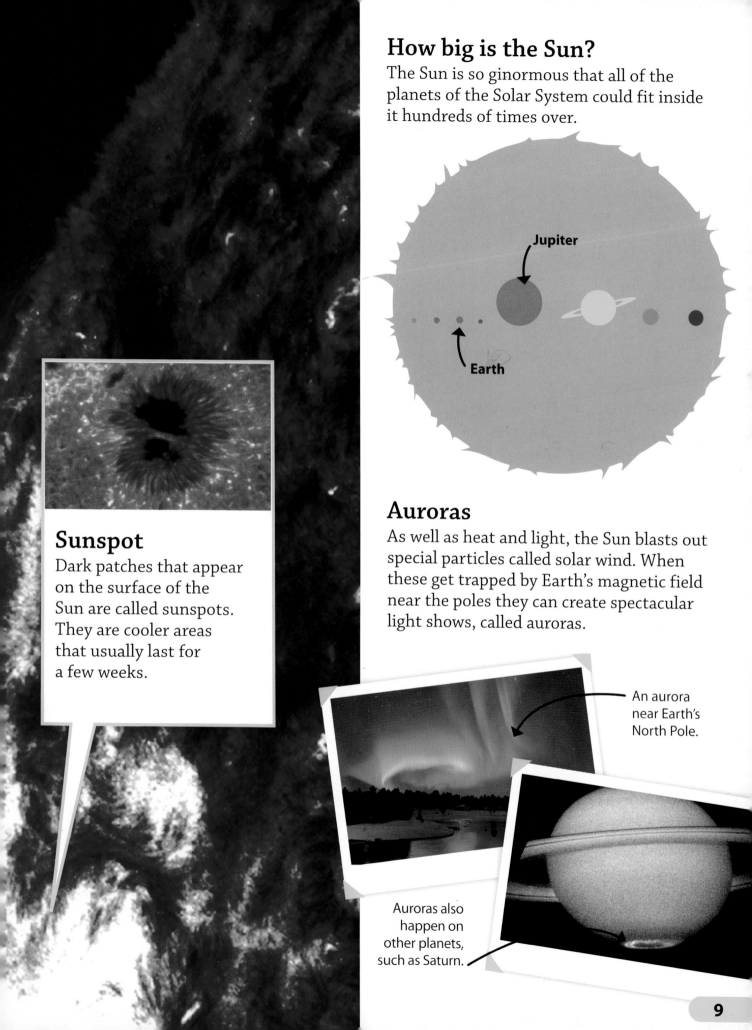

Jupiter

Earth

Sunspot

Dark patches that appear on the surface of the Sun are called sunspots. They are cooler areas that usually last for a few weeks.

Auroras

As well as heat and light, the Sun blasts out special particles called solar wind. When these get trapped by Earth's magnetic field near the poles they can create spectacular light shows, called auroras.

An aurora near Earth's North Pole.

Auroras also happen on other planets, such as Saturn.

Mercury

Mercury is the closest planet to the Sun and the least explored of the four inner rocky planets. Its surface is covered in greyish-brown dust and looks similar to our Moon, with lots of craters where it has been hit by space rocks. Scientists think there is no possibility of life here.

Day: 427°C (801°F)

Night: -173°C (-279°F)

Extreme temperatures

Mercury is a world of extreme temperatures. By day it is scorching hot, but at night it is very cold.

Smallest planet

Mercury is the smallest of the eight planets in our Solar System – it is only slightly bigger than the Earth's Moon.

The Moon

3,476 km (2,160 miles)

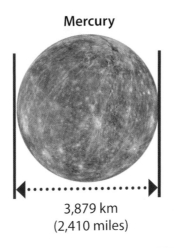

Mercury

3,879 km (2,410 miles)

What's inside?

Mercury has a rocky surface, but inside is a very large metallic core, part of which is molten (liquid).

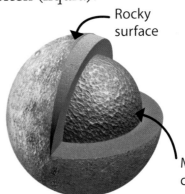

Rocky surface

Metallic core

Planet-gazing

People have been observing Mercury for a very long time, but nobody knows who discovered it. Sometimes it can be seen from Earth around sunset and sunrise.

Mercury at sunset

Impact craters of different sizes.

These **craters** on Mercury look just like **Mickey Mouse!**

FACT FILE

» **Name:** Mercury

» **Number of moons:** 0

» **Distance from Sun:** 57.9 million km (36 million miles)

» **Length of year:** 88 Earth days

Planets to spot

When viewed from Earth, planets can be spotted because they don't twinkle like stars.

Venus
Venus is the brightest of all the planets seen from Earth.

Mars
Mars appears a pale red colour in the night's sky.

Jupiter
Using a small telescope you can see some of Jupiter's moons!

Saturn
With a small telescope you can see Saturn's rings.

Visible at night

Mercury is not the only planet that can be seen with the naked eye. The others are Venus, Mars, Jupiter, and Saturn.

Even binoculars will give you a clear view of Mercury!

Volcanoes

Venus is covered in volcanoes. There is evidence that some may still be erupting.

Barren surface

There are no rivers or lakes on the surface of Venus. The only rain it gets is acid rain that would burn through your skin.

Toxic clouds

Venus is covered in clouds of sulphuric acid. The atmosphere is so thick it would crush you in seconds.

Earth's evil twin

Earth and Venus are about the same size, and are made up of similar rocky materials, but that's where the similarities end! Venus is a deadly world. It's boiling hot, covered in volcanoes, and cloaked in an atmosphere of deadly poisonous gases.

REALLY?

Venus is the **hottest** planet in the **Solar System**.

Atmosphere
Earth's atmosphere protects it from dangerous space radiation, and contains gases like oxygen that we need to breathe.

Life
Earth is home to an amazing variety of plants and animals.

Water
About 71 per cent of Earth's surface is covered by water. It is a vital ingredient for life.

Temperature
With its distance from the Sun, Earth is the perfect temperature for life – neither too hot or too cold.

Life on Earth

Although there may be life elsewhere in our Solar System, we haven't discovered it yet. The only place we know has life for sure is Earth. Our home planet is at just the right distance from our Sun for liquid water to exist, and has all the other key ingredients to make life possible.

Recipe for life
In the mixing bowl are the key ingredients needed for life as we know it:

You will need:
- Raw materials, such as oxygen, nitrogen, and carbon
- Liquid water
- Energy

Raw materials
The raw materials needed for life are found all over Earth – for example in soil. However soil needs water and energy from the Sun before life can appear.

What are we made of?

From the biggest whale in the ocean to a tiny mouse, all life on Earth has one thing in common – it is all made from the same stuff.

It may not look like a whale, but a mouse is made of the same raw materials.

Water
Liquid water is essential for life. It allows crucial changes to take place between raw materials.

Energy
Life on Earth would not be possible without a constant source of energy, such as the Sun.

Stardust

Nearly everything that makes up our bodies, and everything else on Earth, was created when dying stars exploded. These explosions send raw materials like carbon and oxygen hurtling across space, and these raw materials are what we are made of. That means that you are made of stardust!

Stardust from an exploding star.

The Moon

The Moon is our closest neighbour and the only place in the Solar System, other than Earth, that humans have set foot on. The Moon is desert-like, with plains, mountains and valleys, and a black sky. It is covered with craters, because there is no atmosphere to protect it from space rocks.

Moon landings

Twelve people have walked on the Moon, the first being Neil Armstrong. People have driven cars on the Moon, called Lunar Rovers, and even played golf!

Apollo 16 landing module

FACT FILE

» **Average distance from Earth:** 384,400 km (238,900 miles)

» **Surface temperature:** -153°C (-243°F) to 123°C (253°F)

» **Time to orbit Earth:** 27.3 days

» **Age:** 4.5 billion years

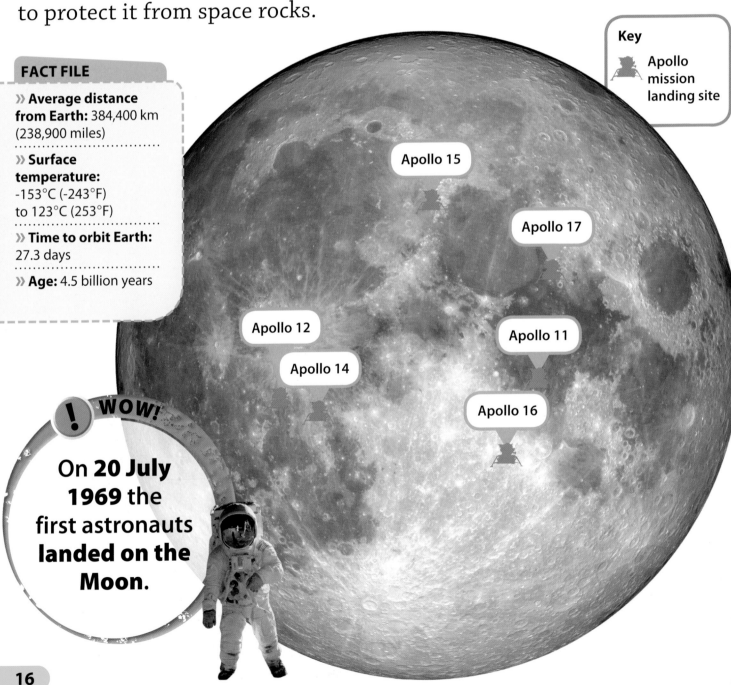

Key

Apollo mission landing site

Apollo 15

Apollo 17

Apollo 12

Apollo 14

Apollo 11

Apollo 16

! WOW!

On **20 July 1969** the first astronauts **landed on the Moon.**

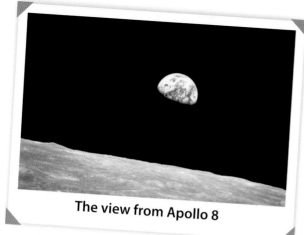
The view from Apollo 8

Moon exploration

People last visited the Moon in 1972, but the footprints they left will last for millions of years because there is no wind to blow them away. This means future Moon explorers will be able to see them.

Footprint on the surface of the Moon

Earthrise

This is the view of Earth as seen from Apollo 8, which was the first manned mission to orbit the Moon. The photograph was taken on Christmas Eve 1968.

Solar eclipse

Sometimes when the Moon passes between the Earth and the Sun, the Moon briefly blocks out light from the Sun, causing an eclipse to be seen on Earth.

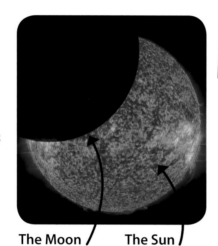
The Moon / The Sun

Mining the Moon

In the future there could be a Moon base, where people could live. Some scientists are even interested in mining the Moon for resources they could turn into rocket fuel.

How the Moon formed

Scientists think the Moon was formed when the Solar System was very young and an object about the size of Mars collided with the young Earth. They think the Moon is debris from the collision, pulled together in Earth's orbit by gravity.

Object collides with Earth   Debris orbits Earth

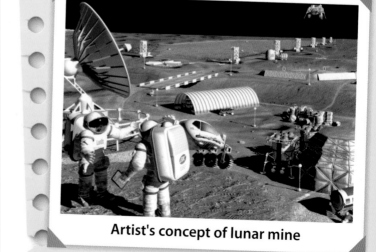
Artist's concept of lunar mine

The Space Race

In the middle of the 20th century the USA and the Soviet Union were struggling to be the most powerful country in the world. Both countries wanted to be the first to send spacecraft and people into space, and so the Space Race began.

USA

Soviet Union

I'm about to em-bark!

The DK Herald
RUSSIANS WIN RACE TO LAUNCH SATELLITE

The first man-made object to travel into space was the Soviet satellite Sputnik 1. It was launched on 4 October 1957.

A month later, on 3 November 1957, the Soviet Union sent a dog into space. She was called Laika, and became the first living creature to orbit the Earth.

But the Soviet Union sent a human to space first! On 12 April 1961, Russian cosmonaut Yuri Gagarin orbited the Earth.

In April 1959, the US introduced its first group of astronauts, known as the Mercury 7. They were an elite group of pilots who did special training to travel to space.

In September 1962, US President John F. Kennedy set the goal of landing a man on the Moon by the end of the decade.

We choose to go to the Moon!

First woman in space

But the Soviets were still ahead, and in June 1963, Valentina Tereshkova became the first woman to travel to space.

In a further triumph, on 18 March 1965 the Soviet cosmonaut Alexei Leonov became the first person to walk in space!

First spacewalk

We have lift off!

However, the United States were first to the Moon. The Apollo 11 mission launched on 16 July 1969 and successfully landed on the Moon four days later.

That's one small step for [a] man, one giant leap for mankind.

On 20 July 1969, Neil Armstrong and Buzz Aldrin (shown here) became the first people to walk on the Moon. The Space Race was over.

Robonaut

Robonaut 2 is a NASA (US space agency) robot astronaut that lives on the space station and helps the crew with simple tasks, such as changing air filters. Its head has cameras, which work like eyes, and its hands can operate simple tools.

Experiments

Astronauts do lots of scientific experiments on the space station to help us understand more about the effects of living in space. This will be useful knowledge for future deep-space exploration.

Canadarm2 is a robotic arm that moves equipment around the ISS.

Science experiments are carried out in the Columbus laboratory.

Living in space

The International Space Station (ISS) is the biggest object ever flown in space. It orbits at around 400 km (250 miles) above Earth and a team of astronauts have lived and worked here since the year 2000. It is our first step towards exploring deeper into the Solar System.

Keeping fit

There is no gravity in space, so astronauts exercise every day. It keeps them healthy and stops their muscles from getting weak.

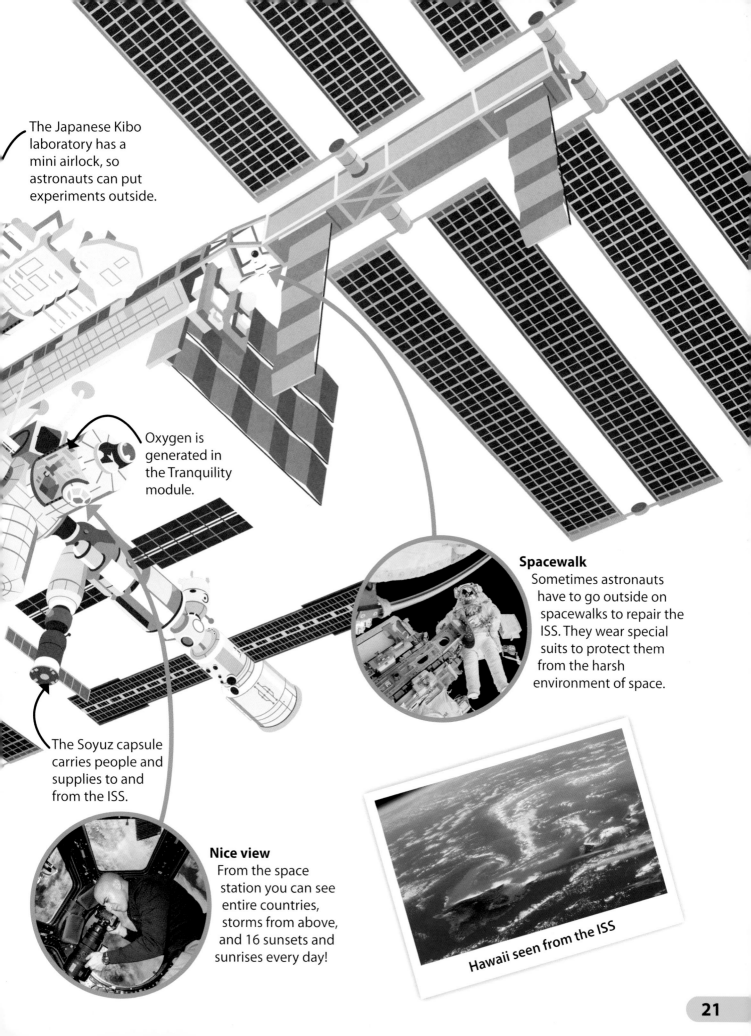

The Japanese Kibo laboratory has a mini airlock, so astronauts can put experiments outside.

Oxygen is generated in the Tranquility module.

Spacewalk
Sometimes astronauts have to go outside on spacewalks to repair the ISS. They wear special suits to protect them from the harsh environment of space.

The Soyuz capsule carries people and supplies to and from the ISS.

Nice view
From the space station you can see entire countries, storms from above, and 16 sunsets and sunrises every day!

Hawaii seen from the ISS

Helmet

Astronauts see out of a clear plastic bubble, and also have a visor to protect them from the Sun's harmful rays.

Display unit

Astronauts operate their life support system using controls on their display unit.

Lots of layers

Spacesuits have 14 layers of material to help keep astronauts safe. Some of these layers protect them from dangerous objects that fly through space.

Life support system

Worn like a backpack, the life support system contains oxygen for the astronaut to breathe, and a battery for electrical power.

Gloves

Spacesuit gloves have heaters in the fingertips to stop an astronaut's fingers from getting cold!

Spacesuit

In outer space there is no air to breathe and the temperature can quickly change from being very hot to very cold. To survive astronauts must wear spacesuits. They are like an astronaut's personal spacecraft, allowing them to do important jobs – such as repairing the space station.

Boots

Astronauts can attach their boots to special foot restraints on the space station to make working in space easier.

Flying free

This space jetpack is called a "Manned Maneuvering Unit". It was used by astronauts in the 1980s to travel in space without being tied to their spacecraft. Today, astronauts have smaller versions in case of emergencies.

WOW!

In 1971, astronaut Al Worden performed a spacewalk on his way back from the Moon!

What's it like to be an astronaut?

Dr Piers Sellers is a British-American NASA astronaut and climate scientist. In his space career he made three Space Shuttle flights. He completed six spacewalks, during which he helped to build the International Space Station!

FACT FILE

» **Name:** Dr Piers Sellers

» **Born:** 1955

» **Space missions:**
• 2002 – Space Shuttle *Atlantis*
• 2006 – Space Shuttle *Discovery*
• 2010 – Space Shuttle *Atlantis*

» **Total time in space:** 35 days

Space Shuttle
The last Space Shuttle flight took place in 2011.

Piers with the rest of the crew of the Space Shuttle *Discovery*

"Space is the new frontier. It is to us what the oceans were to sailors a thousand years ago. We have to cross space to get to the planets in our Solar System. One day, we will travel to planets around other stars. I hope future space explorers will travel to Mars, then the moons of the outer planets."

On board the International Space Station (ISS).

"Zero-G is great fun. You can float through the air down the big main corridor of the space station. It's like magic. But the view of Earth is the main thing. From the ISS you can see over 1,000 miles in all directions – beautiful."

The view from the ISS

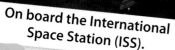

Piers and his crewmates try to get some sleep on board the Space Shuttle *Atlantis*

"It's hard to sleep in space. When you close your eyes you feel like you are falling and so you wake up! You can't shower in zero-G – the water would go everywhere. So you wipe yourself down with a wet washcloth, which works ok. The loo works using an air suction fan to make everything go where it's supposed to go, and that works fine, too!"

"The best part of being an astronaut is spacewalking. Being outside the spacecraft you have a beautiful all-round view of the Earth and space."

Piers on a spacewalk outside the ISS

Spacewalking
Spacewalks can be very tiring. For this one Piers was outside for more than 7 hours!

How do you become an astronaut?

"Currently, you have to be one of the following to be a professional astronaut: military test pilot, engineer, medical doctor, or scientist. So study hard on the STEM subjects [science, technology, engineering, and mathematics] at school. They are hard to begin with, but fascinating and worthwhile."

Professional astronauts
Before becoming astronauts Sunita Williams trained as a pilot and Joan Higginbotham was a engineer.

Mars

Mars is nicknamed the Red Planet because of its rusty soil. Like Earth, it has a rocky surface, polar ice caps, mountains, valleys, and clouds in the sky. However, the fourth planet from the Sun has a far more extreme environment than ours. It is very cold and dry with a thin unbreathable atmosphere.

FACT FILE

» **Name:** Mars

» **Distance from Sun:**
228 million km
(142 million miles)

» **Average temperature:**
-63°C (-81°F)

» **Time to orbit the Sun:**
687 days

» **Number of moons:** 2

Mars' moons

Mars has two moons, called Phobos and Deimos, which are much smaller than Earth's Moon. Their names mean "panic" and "fear". They were probably asteroids pulled towards Mars by its gravity.

Phobos

Deimos

Olympus Mons

Towering high above the Martian landscape is Olympus Mons. It is the largest volcano in our Solar System and nearly three times as high as Mount Everest!

Olympus Mons
25,000 m/82,020 ft

Mount Everest
8,848 m/29,028 ft

Weather on Mars

Like Earth, Mars has seasons. This is because the planets are tilted at similar angles. Different parts of the planet lean towards the Sun at different times during the year, making it warmer or cooler.

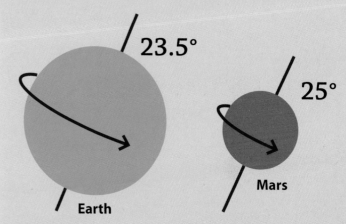

23.5°

25°

Earth

Mars

At an angle
Mars is tilted just 1.5° more than Earth, so it has a similar range of seasons. Seasons on Mars last longer because it takes longer for Mars to travel around the Sun.

Dust devil

Valles Marineris

Valles Marineris is a 4,000 km (2,500 mile) crack across the surface of Mars, at parts 7 km (4 miles) deep. It is a system of canyons, including the vast Coprates Chasma.

Coprates Chasma

Dust storms
On Mars there are huge dust storms that last for weeks. So much dust is kicked up that they can be seen by telescopes on Earth!

A whirlwind on Mars is known as a "dust devil".

Exploring Mars

Scientists have always longed to explore Mars. They believe that in the past the Red Planet could have been far warmer and wetter than it is now. There may once have even been life on Mars, and tiny life forms, such as bacteria, could live on the planet today. Many spacecraft have already visited Mars and in the future humans will too.

! WOW!

The **Curiosity Rover** travels at just **3.8 cm (1.5 in)** per second.

Water on Mars

In 2015, NASA found the strongest evidence yet that liquid water exists on Mars. This was a hugely exciting discovery because scientists looking for life in our Solar System think that where there is liquid water, there could be life.

These channels in the rock suggest water may have flowed here.

Newton Crater

Curiosity Rover

This photo of the Curiosity Rover was taken on the surface of Mars. The six-wheeled, car-sized robot lives and works on the planet, operated by a team of scientists back on Earth. Their instructions take about 15 minutes to reach Mars!

Curiosity has 17 cameras on board. As well as taking photos, this camera can fire a laser to clean away dust from Martian rocks!

Curiosity's robotic arm holds tools for examining the surface.

Wide, grippy wheels help the rover travel over bumpy terrain.

Human exploration

One day people will walk on Mars. Astronauts will see the landscape with their own eyes and become the first humans to walk on another planet. Even if no life is found, reaching Mars will be a crucial step on the way to exploring the wider Solar System.

Maybe you could go to Mars one day...

Artist's impression of humans on Mars

Asteroid belt

Between the planets Mars and Jupiter lies the asteroid belt. It is home to tens of thousands of asteroids. These rocky objects are leftovers from the early Solar System, and are too small to be considered planets. They come in different shapes and sizes with the smallest being less than 1 km (0.6 miles) wide. Some asteroids have moons and one even has rings!

! WOW!

One day **asteroids** could be **mined** for **precious metals** and **water**, to be turned into **rocket fuel.**

Vesta

Craters
These craters are nicknamed "Snowman" because they look just like a snowman! They are on Vesta, one of the largest asteroids in the asteroid belt.

Asteroid orbits

Not all of the asteroids in our Solar System are found in the asteroid belt. Some asteroids pass near other planets, including Earth. Asteroids that come close to Earth are called Near Earth Objects. The planet Jupiter even shares its orbit around the Sun with two groups of asteroids, which are called Trojans.

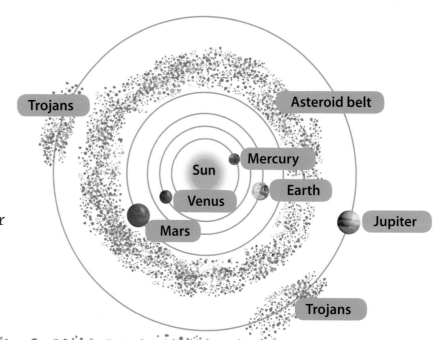

Trojans

Asteroid belt

Sun

Mercury

Earth

Venus

Mars

Jupiter

Trojans

Ceres

By far the largest object in the asteroid belt is Ceres. Made mostly of rock and ice, it was the first asteroid ever discovered. It has since been classed as a Dwarf Planet, because it is more like a planet than its neighbours in the main asteroid belt.

Ceres

Earth's Moon

Ceres

3,476 km (2,160 miles)

950 km (590 miles)

Jupiter

Jupiter is the fifth planet from the Sun and the largest planet in the Solar System. It is a gas giant with thick bands of brown, yellow, and white clouds. Its atmosphere is made up of hydrogen and helium gas, just like our Sun, and if it was much more massive, it could become a star!

! WOW!

Jupiter acts like a **cosmic vacuum cleaner** by sucking up dangerous asteroids!

FACT FILE

» **Name:** Jupiter

» **Average distance from Sun:** 778 million km (484 million miles)

» **Number of known moons:** 67

» **Average temperature:** -145°C (-234°F) to 24,000°C (43,000°F)

Giant planet

Jupiter is the king of the Solar System. It is an amazing 143,000 km (89,000 miles) wide. Jupiter is so large that all of the other planets could fit inside it!

Juno mission

NASA's Juno spacecraft is helping scientists to understand how Jupiter formed. It is orbiting closer to the gas giant than any spacecraft has before.

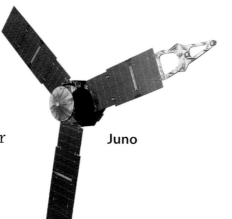

Juno

Beneath the clouds

Any spacecraft that passed through Jupiter's clouds would be crushed and melted by the huge pressure. Scientists believe that beneath the clouds there is a giant ocean made of liquid metal.

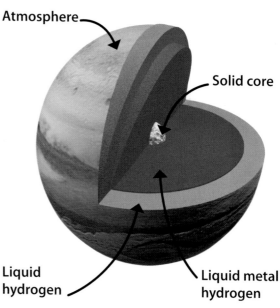

Atmosphere

Solid core

Liquid hydrogen

Liquid metal hydrogen

Jupiter's rings

Jupiter has three thin rings, called the Jovian Rings. They are mostly made of dust and can only be seen when viewed from behind Jupiter, when they are lit up by the Sun.

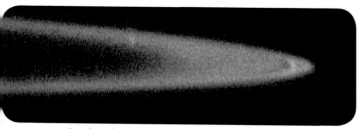

Jupiter's rings photographed by the New Horizons spacecraft in 2007.

Great Red Spot

One of Jupiter's most famous features is the Great Red Spot. It is a huge storm, more than three times the size of Earth, that has been raging for hundreds of years!

Jupiter's moons

Jupiter's four largest moons were the first moons to be discovered orbiting another planet. They are incredible worlds of volcanoes, craters, and hidden oceans that have barely been explored. Some could even be home to alien life!

Io

Io is similar in size to the Earth's Moon. Chemicals from volcanic eruptions have turned its surface yellow-orange.

Europa

Europa is the smallest of Jupiter's four largest moons. On the surface there is water ice and underneath scientists believe there is an ocean!

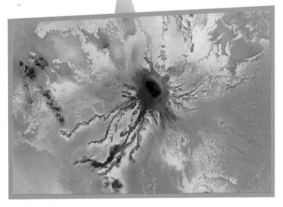

Volcanic moon
Io is the most volcanically active world in our Solar System. Hundreds of volcanoes spew lava thousands of metres into the air.

Ice geysers
Gigantic jets of water are thought to spout from geysers on Europa's icy surface. These fountains may be up to 20 times higher than Mount Everest!

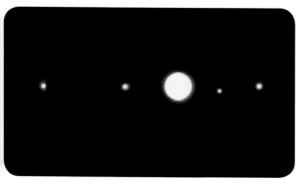

In the night sky

If you look at Jupiter through a telescope you might see bright lights hovering next to the planet. These are actually its four largest moons!

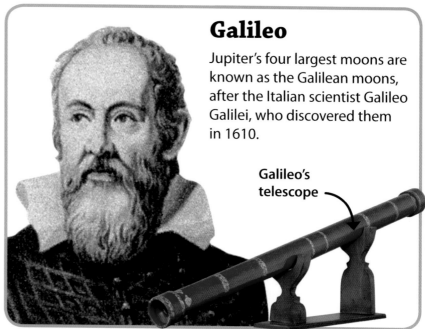

Galileo

Jupiter's four largest moons are known as the Galilean moons, after the Italian scientist Galileo Galilei, who discovered them in 1610.

Galileo's telescope

Ganymede

The largest moon in our Solar System, Ganymede is even bigger than the planet Mercury! It is made of rock and ice.

Callisto

This battered moon has more craters than any other object in the whole Solar System!

In orbit

With at least 67 moons, Jupiter is almost like its own mini Solar System. Io is the closest of the four largest moons and takes 42 hours to orbit around the planet. Callisto, the furthest away, takes around seventeen days to complete its orbit.

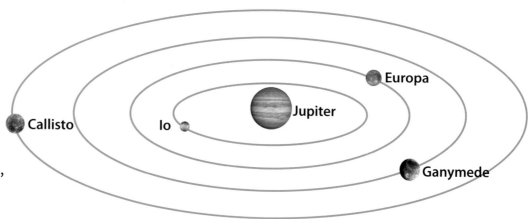

Callisto
Io
Jupiter
Europa
Ganymede

Saturn

Saturn is the second largest planet, after Jupiter, and is known as the "Jewel of the Solar System" because of its spectacular rings. It is a gas giant that spins so fast it bulges out in the middle.

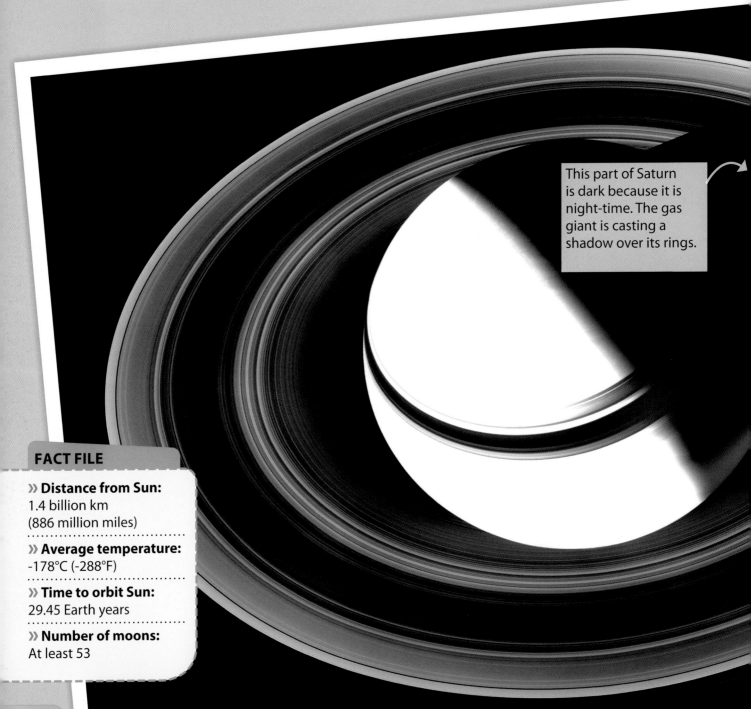

This part of Saturn is dark because it is night-time. The gas giant is casting a shadow over its rings.

FACT FILE

» **Distance from Sun:**
1.4 billion km
(886 million miles)

» **Average temperature:**
-178°C (-288°F)

» **Time to orbit Sun:**
29.45 Earth years

» **Number of moons:**
At least 53

Bathtime

Despite its mammoth size, Saturn isn't very dense. This means that if you could build a gigantic bath, Saturn would float in it!

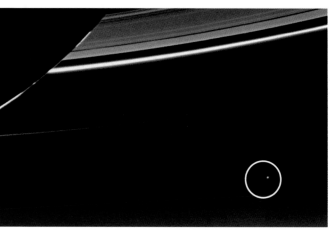

Earth as seen from Saturn.

Cassini-
Huygens
probe

A view of home

The tiny blue dot in the bottom right of this picture is where you live. This picture of our home planet was taken by NASA's Cassini-Huygens spacecraft when it visited Saturn in 2004.

Lord of the rings

Saturn is surrounded by rings that are made up of billions of chunks of rock and ice. The rings can be seen from Earth through a telescope.

Ice giants

Cold and dark, Uranus and Neptune are known as ice giants because they are made of a mix of gas and icy materials. Both worlds have small rings and many moons. They have only been visited by one spacecraft, Voyager 2, and are still waiting to be explored.

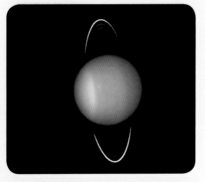

Uranus has 13 known rings.

! WOW!

Most of **Uranus' moons** are named after **characters** in **Shakespeare** plays, for example **Puck** and **Miranda**.

Spinning on its side

Uranus is the odd-ball of the Solar System, as it orbits the Sun tilted on its side! Scientists think this is because Uranus was struck by an Earth-sized object early in its life, knocking it over.

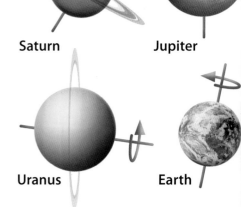

Saturn

Jupiter

Uranus

Earth

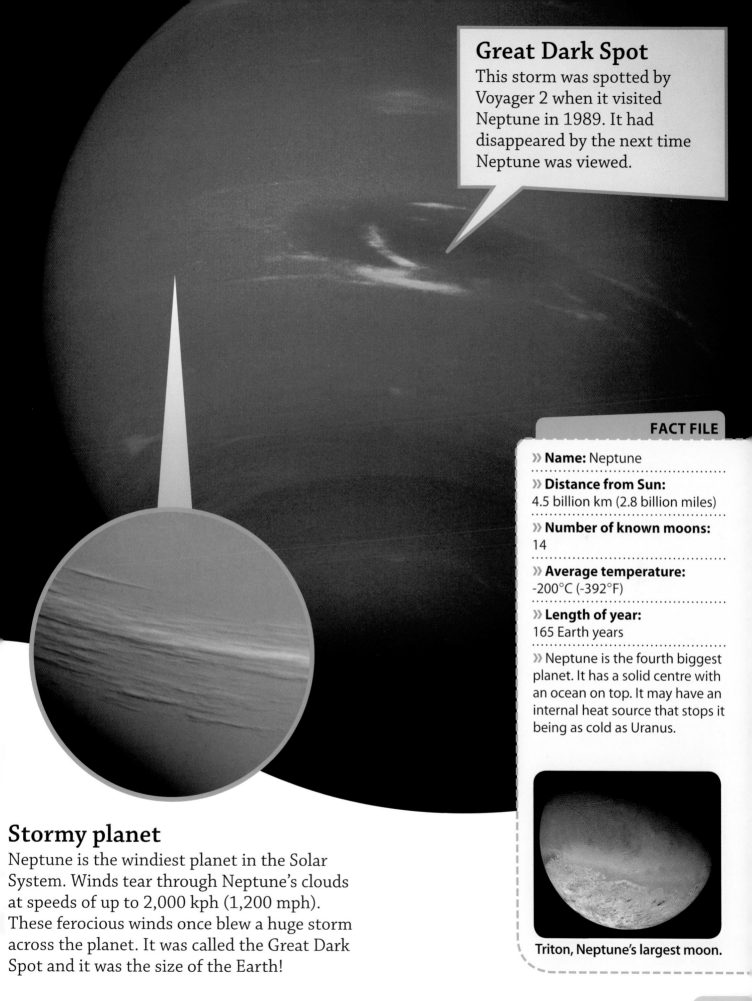

Great Dark Spot
This storm was spotted by Voyager 2 when it visited Neptune in 1989. It had disappeared by the next time Neptune was viewed.

FACT FILE
» **Name:** Neptune

» **Distance from Sun:**
4.5 billion km (2.8 billion miles)

» **Number of known moons:**
14

» **Average temperature:**
-200°C (-392°F)

» **Length of year:**
165 Earth years

» Neptune is the fourth biggest planet. It has a solid centre with an ocean on top. It may have an internal heat source that stops it being as cold as Uranus.

Triton, Neptune's largest moon.

Stormy planet
Neptune is the windiest planet in the Solar System. Winds tear through Neptune's clouds at speeds of up to 2,000 kph (1,200 mph). These ferocious winds once blew a huge storm across the planet. It was called the Great Dark Spot and it was the size of the Earth!

Pluto

Pluto was once thought to be a barren, boring lump of rock at the edge of the Solar System. However, a recent mission has shed new light on this mysterious world. It is filled with ice mountains and volcanoes, and it has particles in its atmosphere that scatter sunlight, giving it a blue sky just like on Earth.

Craters on Pluto's ice plains

Ice mountains

FACT FILE

» **Name:** Pluto

» **Average distance from Sun:**
5.9 billion km
(3.67 billion miles)

» **Surface temperature:**
-233°C (-387°F)

» **Time to orbit Sun:**
246 Earth years

» **Number of moons:**
5

Strange surface

In 2015, photos revealed Pluto's surface for the first time. NASA scientists spotted smooth plains riddled with craters and mountains of ice.

Dwarf planets

In 2006 it was decided Pluto wasn't a planet, but a dwarf planet. Dwarf planets are similar to planets in many ways, but share their orbits around the Sun with other objects, such as asteroids and comets. There are currently five recognized dwarf planets in the Solar System, but it is thought there are many more.

Earth   **Ceres**   **Pluto**   **Eris**   **Makemake**   **Haumea**

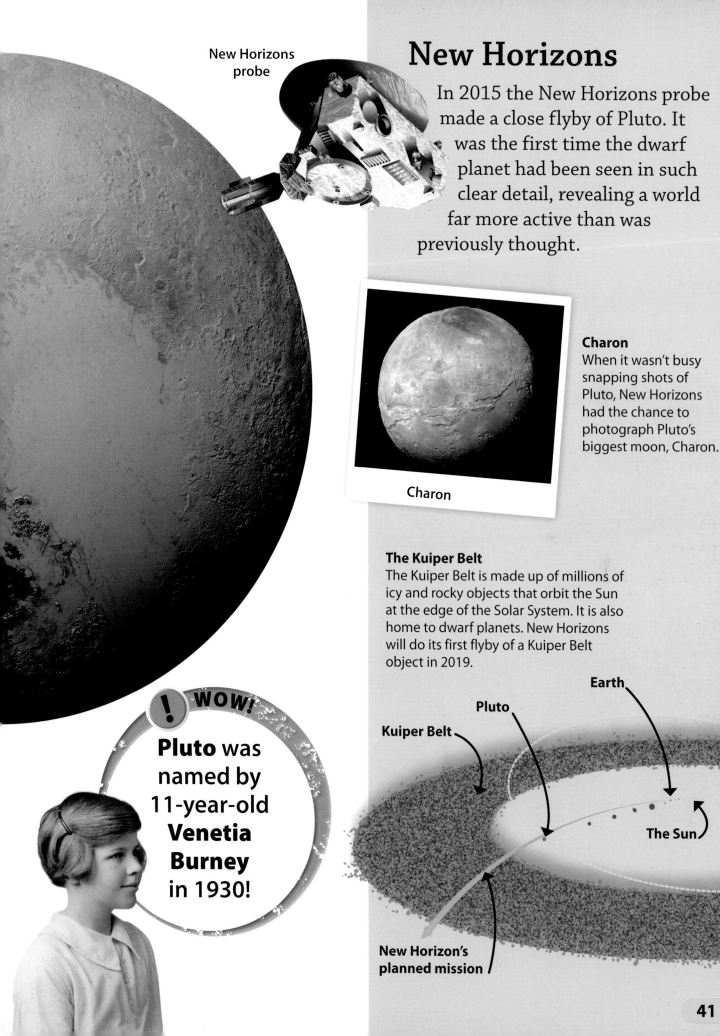

New Horizons probe

New Horizons

In 2015 the New Horizons probe made a close flyby of Pluto. It was the first time the dwarf planet had been seen in such clear detail, revealing a world far more active than was previously thought.

Charon
When it wasn't busy snapping shots of Pluto, New Horizons had the chance to photograph Pluto's biggest moon, Charon.

Charon

The Kuiper Belt
The Kuiper Belt is made up of millions of icy and rocky objects that orbit the Sun at the edge of the Solar System. It is also home to dwarf planets. New Horizons will do its first flyby of a Kuiper Belt object in 2019.

Earth

Pluto

Kuiper Belt

The Sun

New Horizon's planned mission

! WOW!

Pluto was named by 11-year-old **Venetia Burney** in 1930!

Meet the expert

Dr Alan Stern is an engineer, planetary scientist, and space explorer. He led the first ever mission to visit Pluto, a probe called New Horizons. His team are now using the spacecraft to study other worlds in the Kuiper Belt.

Alan aged 6

Q: What inspired you as a child?

A: I was a little boy at the start of the space program [in the 1960s] and then as a teenager I saw people regularly walk on the Moon. I wanted to be a part of the future of space exploration.

Q: How does it feel to lead the first mission to Pluto?

A: Pluto was the only one of the classical planets not explored [Pluto was still classified as a planet when New Horizons launched in 2006]. To be able to lead the exploration of the furthest planet that was known is a privilege. Feels like a dream! This was a big team effort by people who worked for 15 years to see Pluto explored. Humans have finally completed the first exploration of our Solar System. It is inspirational and shows people we can do great things in our time.

Q: Why did people want to go to Pluto?

A: In the 1990s we discovered the Kuiper Belt and this gave us a context for Pluto. Before that we just had four rocky planets, four gas planets, and then Pluto out on the edge – it was a bit of a misfit. We discovered many other small planets and realized Pluto was the first of a whole new class of small planets.

Mystery world
Before New Horizons the only images of Pluto were very blurry.

Image of Pluto from 2003.

Mystery solved
New Horizons sent back amazing photos revealing the surface of Pluto.

Q: How hard was it to send a spacecraft to Pluto?

A: Very hard. It was a decade long flight to get to Pluto and we had no second chance if we missed the flyby. We had to get it right on the first try and be prepared to get it right. The pioneers of space exploration had developed the technology to do this. The only exception was new technology to miniaturize the science experiments [to make sure New Horizons wasn't too heavy].

Q: How do you feel about Pluto being reclassified as a dwarf planet?

A: I think it was a huge mistake. At the time of the flyby it became obvious that it is clearly a planet and not something else. It has the properties of a planet and the images we have got back from New Horizons demonstrate this. Pluto has properties similar to the terrestrial [rocky] planets. And in my view it is more of a planet than the gas giants.

Q: How did it feel seeing the first images of Pluto?

A: We had a pretty good idea that Pluto would be complicated. But actually seeing the images – mindblowing! We could see the surface and it was very interesting for scientists. We are learning lots about Pluto. It is geologically active and we don't understand the mechanisms. I felt very happy that the team had succeeded.

Q: Any surprises about Pluto?

A: We discovered that Pluto has parts of its surface that are 4.5 billion years old, other parts that are 1 billion years old,

Alan and his team look at the first photos sent back by New Horizons.

and some parts were only born yesterday. It's a puzzle to us! Pluto also has volcanoes, which rival the big ones on Mars.

Q: What are your favourite planets?

A: Pluto and Earth. Earth is joint favourite because we live here, it gave birth to our species, and it is the only planet where you can take your dog for a walk!

Q: What are your hopes for the future?

A: I hope we continue to accelerate in the field of science and commercial spaceflight. The exploration of space is the most important achievement in the history of humanity. I hope that one day space probes will land on Pluto and humans will explore it in person.

Q: Do you have any advice for future space explorers?

Study hard, work hard, and find your passion!

Name that rock

Space rocks are known by different names, depending on their size.

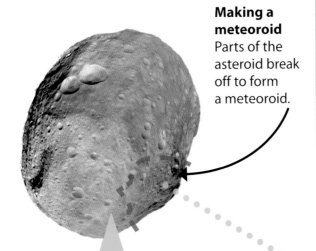

Making a meteoroid
Parts of the asteroid break off to form a meteoroid.

Meteoroid

A small piece of rock or space dust that has broken off an asteroid or comet is called a meteoroid.

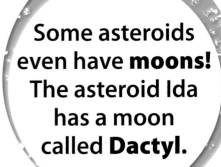

! WOW!

Some asteroids even have **moons!** The asteroid Ida has a moon called **Dactyl.**

Meteor

A meteoroid that burns up as it passes through the Earth's atmosphere is called a meteor. They are also known as "shooting stars".

Asteroid

An asteroid is a rocky object that orbits the Sun. They are much smaller than planets. Some are less than 1 km (0.6 miles) wide.

Space rocks

Our Solar System isn't just made up of planets, dwarf planets, and moons. There are lots of other objects that make up the Solar System family. Comets and asteroids have existed since the Solar System formed, and both have hit Earth in the past. There are also smaller bits of rock and dust, called meteoroids, meteors, and meteorites.

Death of the dinosaurs

Every day around 90 tonnes (100 tons) of rock and dust from space smashes into the Earth. Most of it burns up in the atmosphere, but larger objects can reach the ground. Scientists think a meteorite about 10 km (6 miles) wide hit into the Earth about 65 million years ago, wiping out the dinosaurs.

Meteor Crater, Arizona, USA

Meteorite

If the meteor makes it to the ground it is called a meteorite.

Comets

Made from rock, ice, and dust, comets are the size of mountains. There are thousands of billions of comets in our Solar System.

Comet Hale–Bopp burned brightly enough to be seen from the Earth without a telescope.

Orbiting the Sun

Comets travel around the Sun in an oval-shaped orbit. Some comets are so far away they take tens of millions of years to orbit the Sun.

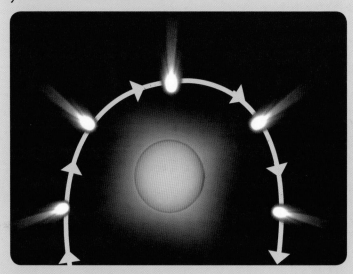

How the tail forms
Comets get tails when they pass near the Sun and are heated up. The tails always point away from the Sun.

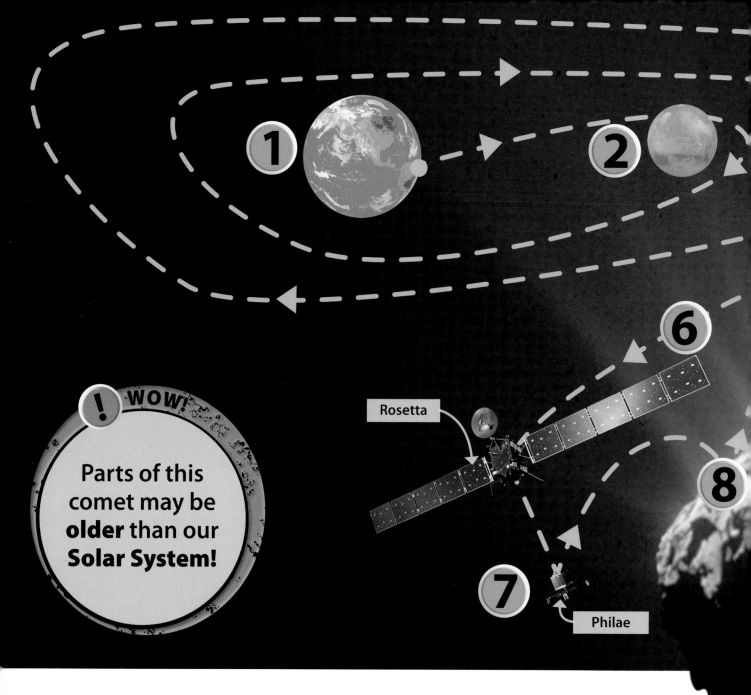

1

2

6

8

7

Rosetta

Philae

! WOW!

Parts of this comet may be **older** than our **Solar System!**

Landing on a comet

The spacecraft Rosetta and its lander Philae travelled for ten years across the Solar System to reach the comet 67P/Churyumov–Gerasimenko. To get enough speed, the spacecraft had to loop around the Earth three times and Mars once, using the gravity of the planets to slingshot through space. On the way they passed lots of other fascinating objects. Finally, in 2014, Philae made the first ever successful touchdown on a comet.

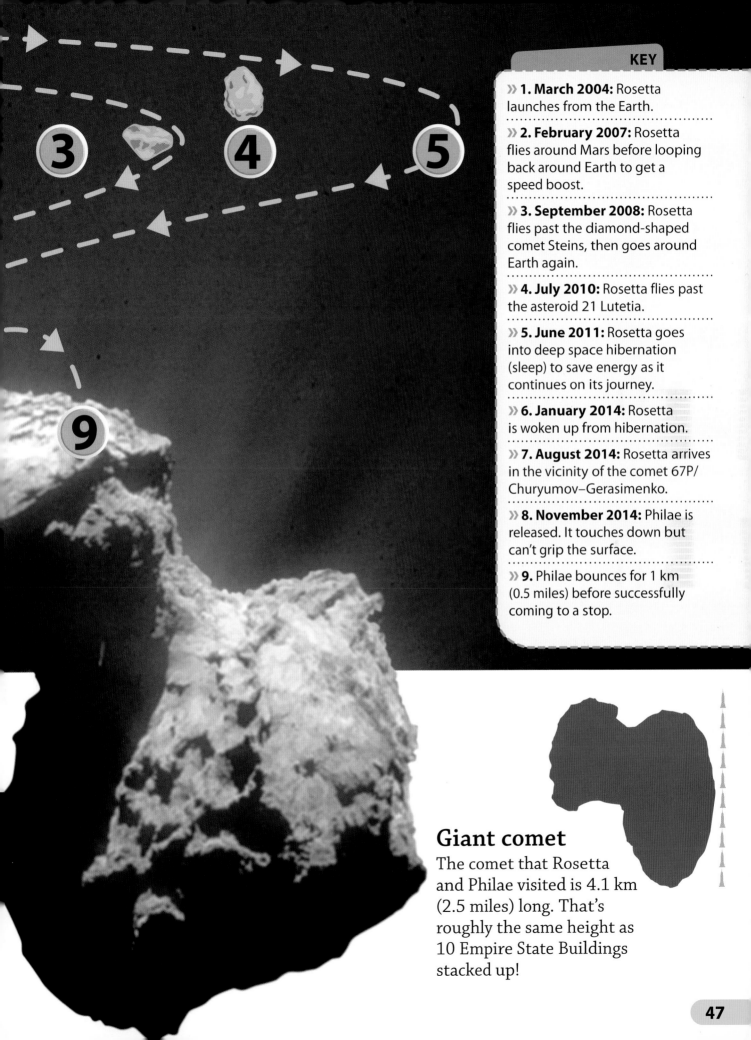

» **1. March 2004:** Rosetta launches from the Earth.

» **2. February 2007:** Rosetta flies around Mars before looping back around Earth to get a speed boost.

» **3. September 2008:** Rosetta flies past the diamond-shaped comet Steins, then goes around Earth again.

» **4. July 2010:** Rosetta flies past the asteroid 21 Lutetia.

» **5. June 2011:** Rosetta goes into deep space hibernation (sleep) to save energy as it continues on its journey.

» **6. January 2014:** Rosetta is woken up from hibernation.

» **7. August 2014:** Rosetta arrives in the vicinity of the comet 67P/Churyumov–Gerasimenko.

» **8. November 2014:** Philae is released. It touches down but can't grip the surface.

» **9.** Philae bounces for 1 km (0.5 miles) before successfully coming to a stop.

Giant comet

The comet that Rosetta and Philae visited is 4.1 km (2.5 miles) long. That's roughly the same height as 10 Empire State Buildings stacked up!

Space ages

Did you know that you are a different age on each planet? This is because a year is the time it takes an object in the Solar System to orbit the Sun. Every planet or dwarf planet takes a different length of time to do this, so their years can be long or short. A year on Earth is the same as about four years on Mercury, while a year on Pluto takes 248 Earth years!

Mercury

Mercury flies round the Sun more quickly than the other planets – its year is only 88 Earth days long. That means that if you are 10 on Earth, you are 41 on Mercury!

A year on **Mercury** is **88** Earth days

A year on **Earth** is **365** Earth days

A year on **Venus** is **225** Earth days

Venus

A day is the amount of time it takes a planet to spin once. Venus takes 225 Earth days to orbit the Sun, but it spins very slowly. This means the days on Venus are very long. In fact, a day on Venus is longer than a year on Venus!

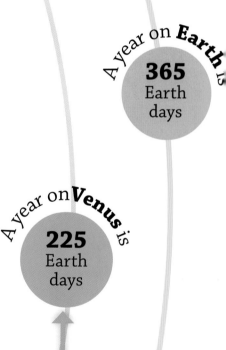

A year on **Uranus** is

84 Earth years

A year on **Jupiter** is

12 Earth years

A year on **Pluto** is

248 Earth years

Pluto

Pluto is so far from the Sun that you would wait a long time for your first birthday. It would take 2,480 Earth years to turn 10!

A year on **Mars** is

687 Earth days

A year on **Saturn** is

29 Earth years

A year on **Neptune** is

165 Earth years

! WOW!

A **90-year-old** on **Earth** is **373 years old** on **Mercury!**

Neptune

A year on Neptune takes 165 Earth years. This means that it is impossible to turn one on Neptune in a human lifetime.

Alien hunters

Are we alone in the Universe? It is one of the great unanswered questions. Some scientists think it is very likely that the Universe is full of life. Their motto is "follow the water", as they believe the best place to find life will be where there is liquid water. Within our own Solar System there are several places of interest to these scientists.

Candidates for life

Although finding intelligent life, like us, in our own Solar System is unlikely, there are worlds that may be home to simple forms of life. Scientists are interested in these places because they have conditions that might be suitable for life to exist.

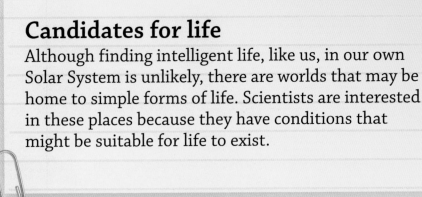

Earth

Sun

Venus

Jupiter

Mars

Europa's ocean is thought to be beneath an ice crust several kilometres thick.

Europa
Scientists believe that there is a liquid water ocean under the thick frozen surface of Jupiter's moon, Europa. Life has been found at the deepest, darkest parts of Earth's oceans, and scientists think the same thing might be possible on Europa.

Mars
Mars is of interest to scientists because of the recent discovery of flowing water on its surface. It is possible that life may have existed on the planet in the past, or that some form of life may still exist today.

Enceladus

Enceladus is a moon that orbits around Saturn. It has a frozen surface and scientists think there is liquid water underneath. The Cassini spacecraft has been flying through geysers of frozen water that erupt from the surface, and analysing it to see if it could harbour life.

Enceladus photographed by Cassini.

Photo of Titan taken by the Huygens probe.

Sunlight reflecting off Titan's seas.

Titan

Titan is Saturn's largest moon. It has a thick atmosphere and seas made of liquid gas. Titan is very interesting to scientists because its atmosphere may be similar to that of the early Earth – before life emerged on our planet.

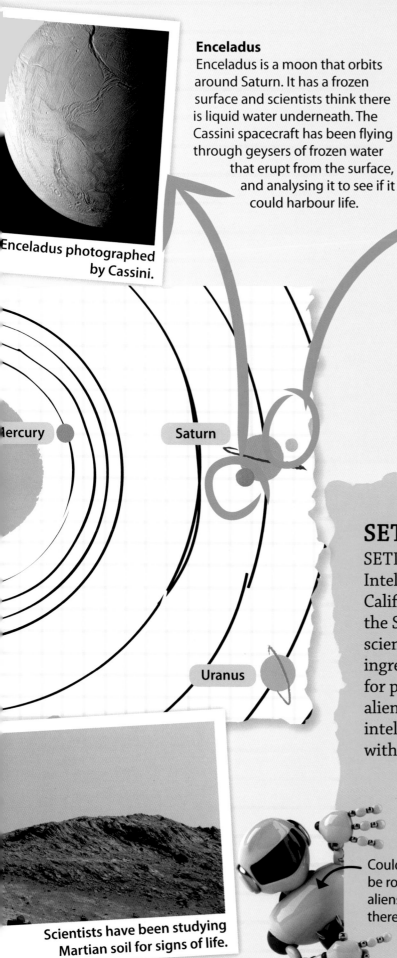

Mercury

Saturn

Uranus

SETI Institute

SETI stands for "Search for Extra Terrestrial Intelligence". The SETI Institute, based in California, USA, is looking for evidence of life in the Solar System and the wider Universe. SETI scientists try to find places that may have the ingredients needed for life and also listen out for possible signals that may have come from aliens. SETI believe our first contact with intelligent life in the Universe may even be with robots built by alien civilizations!

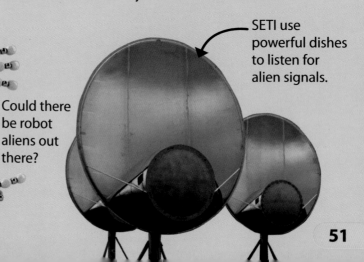

SETI use powerful dishes to listen for alien signals.

Could there be robot aliens out there?

Scientists have been studying Martian soil for signs of life.

Postcards from probes

Voyager 1 and 2 are twin spacecrafts that were launched in the 1970s. Since then they have been on an incredible journey across our Solar System, visiting the planets Jupiter, Saturn, Uranus, and Neptune. The mission was far more successful than scientists had imagined it would be, and the spacecrafts are still sending back information to Earth.

START 5 September 1977 Voyager 1 launches

Jupiter

Voyager 1 and 2 took pictures of Jupiter's Great Red Spot and saw that one of its moons, called Io, has active volcanoes.

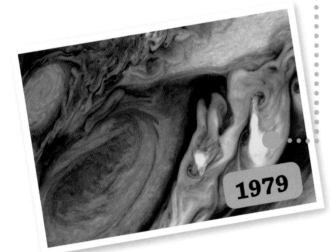
1979

Saturn

Both spacecrafts photographed Saturn's rings and moons. Scientists learned about what Saturn was made of and what its weather was like.

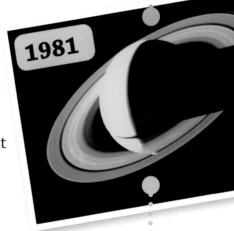
1981

START 20 August 1977 Voyager 2 launches

Uranus

Voyager 2 was the first spacecraft to visit Uranus. It discovered ten new moons around the planet!

1986

Leaving the Solar System

On 25 August 2012, Voyager 1 became the first human-made object to leave the Solar System!

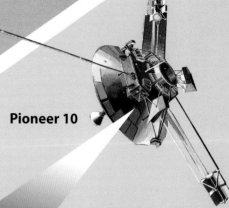

2012

Pioneer 10

Voyager 1 heads towards the far reaches of the Solar System

Pioneer missions

Launched just before the Voyager missions, Pioneer 10 and 11 were the first spacecrafts to cross the asteroid belt and visit Jupiter and Saturn.

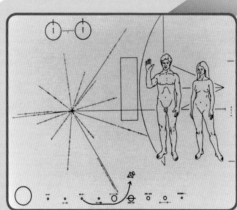

Anyone out there?

In case they are found by aliens, the Pioneer probes carry plaques showing the position of Earth in the Solar System and what humans look like!

Family portrait

The Pioneer project also sent probes to visit the inner planets and to orbit the Earth, some of which launched in the 1950s.

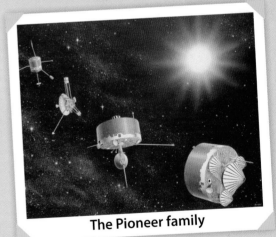

The Pioneer family

Voyager 2 explores the outer planets

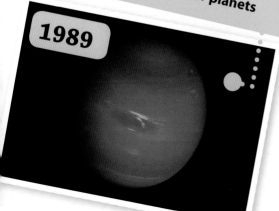

1989

Neptune

In the late 1980s Voyager 2 reached Neptune, the final planet on its tour. It passed close to Neptune's largest moon, called Triton.

The future

The Sun won't last forever. Just like other stars in the Universe, the Sun was born and it will die. At 4.6 billion years old, the Sun is almost halfway through its life. In about 5 billion years time it will start to change, as it burns up the fuel that kept it shining bright for so long. It will expand to become a type of star called a red giant, before shrinking to become a white dwarf.

Life of the Sun

The Sun is a medium-sized star. This diagram shows the life cycle of the Sun – from its birth to when it starts to run out of fuel.

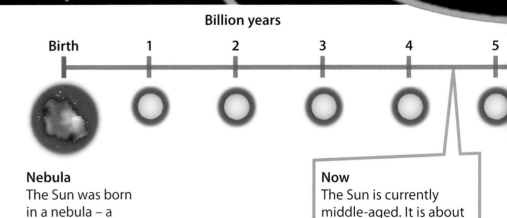

Billion years

Birth   1   2   3   4   5

Nebula
The Sun was born in a nebula – a giant cloud of gas and dust.

Now
The Sun is currently middle-aged. It is about halfway through its life.

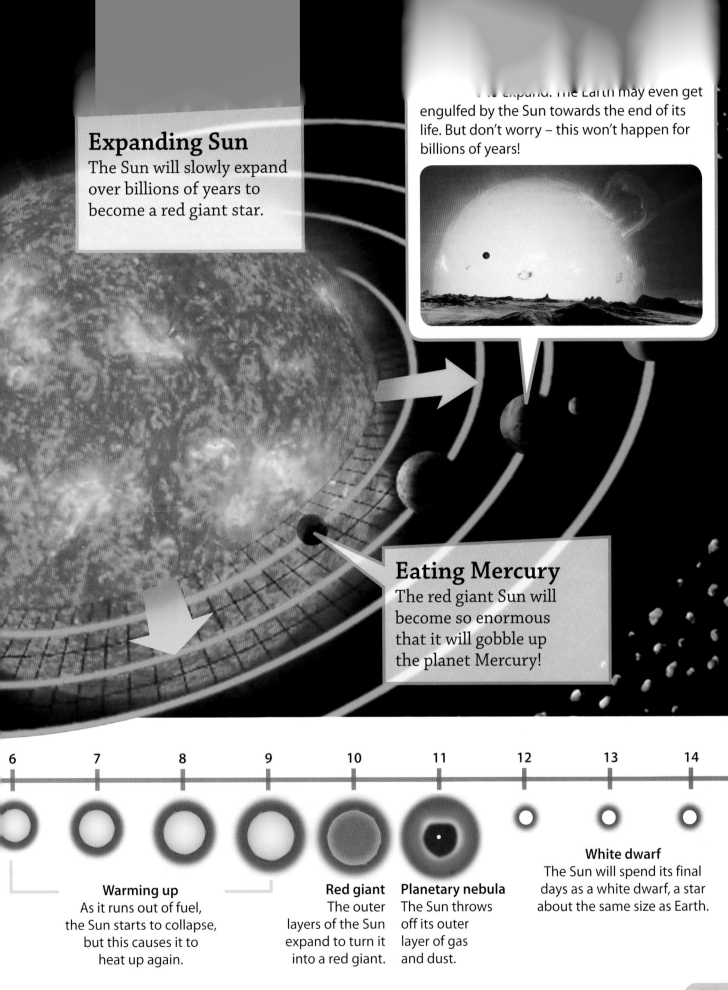

Expanding Sun

The Sun will slowly expand over billions of years to become a red giant star.

...expand. The Earth may even get engulfed by the Sun towards the end of its life. But don't worry – this won't happen for billions of years!

Eating Mercury

The red giant Sun will become so enormous that it will gobble up the planet Mercury!

6   7   8   9   10   11   12   13   14

Warming up
As it runs out of fuel, the Sun starts to collapse, but this causes it to heat up again.

Red giant
The outer layers of the Sun expand to turn it into a red giant.

Planetary nebula
The Sun throws off its outer layer of gas and dust.

White dwarf
The Sun will spend its final days as a white dwarf, a star about the same size as Earth.

Beyond the Solar System

Our Sun is one of many stars in our galaxy and our galaxy, the Milky Way, is one of many galaxies in the Universe. It is not yet possible for humans to travel beyond our Solar System, but by using telescopes scientists are able to take pictures of galaxies trillions and trillions of kilometres away.

Hubble Ultra-Deep Field image

This picture, taken by the Hubble Space Telescope, shows some of the farthest galaxies ever seen. It is just a small section of the night sky and the galaxies you are looking at are nearly as old as the Universe itself!

Looking into deep space

Using space telescopes, scientists have seen stars being born and dying, and observed very distant galaxies. They have been able to work out that the Universe is nearly 14 billion years old.

Section of the night sky

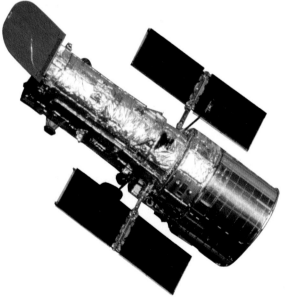

Hubble Telescope

Orbiting above the Earth is the Hubble Space Telescope. The size of a large school bus, it faces out towards space and takes pictures of distant stars and galaxies.

3 AMAZING FACTS

Deep space

1 Scientists estimate that there are at least 100 billion galaxies in the Universe.

2 A typical galaxy, like our home galaxy, the Milky Way, contains hundreds of billions of stars.

3 It would take light 13.2 billion years to reach the furthest galaxy we have detected from Earth.

Each of these specks is a separate galaxy containing billions of stars!

Exoplanets

Our Sun is not the only star that has planets orbiting around it. Lots of other stars have planets, too, and scientists call these "exoplanets".

Kepler-22b

Earth-like

This Earth-like planet was found orbiting around a star nearly 600 light years away from Earth. A light year is the distance light can travel in a year.

Space facts and figures

Space is constantly surprising scientists, even to this day. Here are some weird and wonderful facts you might not know about it!

IT WOULD TAKE MORE THAN **700 YEARS** TO FLY A PLANE TO **PLUTO**.*

*If it were possible!

All of the other planets in the Solar System could fit in the space between the Earth and the Moon!

5

cm (2 in) is how much taller you could be in space due to a lack of gravity.

275 million

The number of new stars formed every day.

The average temperature on the surface of Venus is a sizzling 460°C (860°F).

The Sun weighs **2,000 trillion, trillion tonnes!**
That's about 300,000 times more than the Earth.

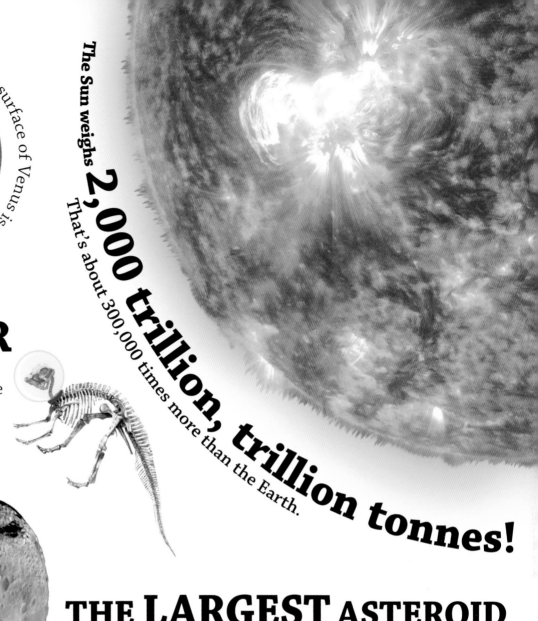

The first DINOSAUR
in orbit was Maiasaura peeblesorum. Its bones were carried to space in 1985!

THE LARGEST ASTEROID
in the Solar System, Vesta, is 525 km (326 miles) wide and has a mountain twice the size of Mount Everest!

Vesta

42
kilometres (26 miles) per second is the top speed meteoroids can travel through space.

536
The number of people who have been into space since Yuri Gagarin in 1961.

1 million
Earths can fit inside the Sun.

Glossary

Here are the meanings of some words that might be useful for you to know when learning about space.

asteroid Small, rocky object that orbits the Sun

asteroid belt Area of the Solar System between Mars and Jupiter containing a large number of asteroids

astronaut Person trained to travel and live in space

atmosphere Layer of gas that surrounds a planet

axis Imaginary line that passes through the centre of a planet or star, around which the planet or star rotates

black hole Object in space with such a strong force of gravity that nothing can escape it, not even light

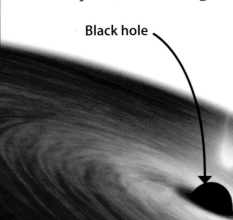

Black hole

capsule Small spacecraft, or part of a larger one, which usually carries crew or scientific instruments

cargo Goods carried on a spacecraft

comet Object made of dust and ice that orbits around the Sun, developing a tail as it gets near to the Sun

core Central part of a star, planet, or moon

crater Bowl-shaped dent on the surface of a planet or other body in space, caused by the collision with a space rock

crew Group of people who work on a spacecraft

crust Outer layer of a rocky planet

debris Broken pieces of rock and other materials in space

eclipse When an object in space passes into the shadow of another object

equator Imaginary line around the middle of a planet, halfway between the north and south poles

exoplanet Planet that orbits a star other than the Sun

galaxy Huge group of stars, gas, and dust held together by gravity

gravity Force that pulls objects towards each other

habitable Suitable for living in or on

hemisphere One half of a planet or moon

laboratory Place where science experiments are done

launch Send something into space

launch vehicle Rocket-powered vehicle used to send spacecraft or satellites into space

light year Distance travelled by light in a year

lunar Word used to relate to the Moon

magnetic field Force field surrounding a planet, star, or galaxy

mantle Thick layer of hot rock between the core and the crust of a planet or moon

meteor When a meteoroid burns up as it enters Earth's atmosphere, appearing as a streak of light

meteorite Meteoroid that lands on a planet or moon's surface

meteoroid Particle of rock, metal, or ice travelling through space

Milky Way Galaxy we live in

module Unit of a spacecraft

moon Object made of rock or rock and ice that orbits a planet or asteroid

nebula Cloud of gas and dust in space where stars are born

orbit Path an object takes around another when pulled by its gravity

particle Extremely small part of a solid, liquid, or gas

planet Large spherical object that orbits a star

probe Unmanned spacecraft designed to study objects in space and send information back to the Earth

red giant Large star with a reddish colour that is nearing the final stages of its life

rover Vehicle that is driven on the surface of a planet or moon

satellite Object that orbits another larger object

solar Word used to relate to the Sun

Solar System The Sun and the planets and other objects that orbit it

space Place beyond Earth's atmosphere

spacecraft Vehicle that travels in space

spacesuit Sealed protective clothing item worn by astronauts outside a spacecraft in space

spacewalk When an astronaut in space is outside a spacecraft, usually to repair or test equipment

star Huge glowing sphere of gas that creates energy in its core

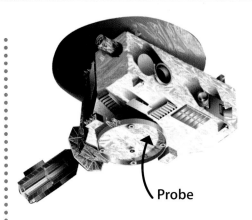

Probe

telescope Instrument used to look at distant objects

Universe All space and everything in it

white dwarf Shrunken star at the end of its life

Spacesuit

Index

Acknowledgements

DORLING KINDERSLEY would like to thank: Emma Chafer for editorial assistance, Hoa Luc for design assistance, Alexandra Beeden for proofreading, Helen Peters for the index, and Daniel Long for his illustrations. The publishers would also like to thank Dr Piers Sellers for his help on "What's it like to be an astronaut?", Dr Alan Stern for the "Meet the expert" interview, and Bill Diamond of the SETI Institute for his help with "Life on Earth" and "Alien Hunters".

The publisher would like to thank the following for their kind permission to reproduce their photographs:

(Key: a-above; b-below/bottom; c-centre; f-far; l-left; r-right; t-top)

2 NASA: (fcrb); JHUAPL / SwRI (bl); JPL / Space Science Institute (bc); Goddard / Lunar Reconnaissance Orbiter (cb). **3 ESA:** ESA 2010 MPS for OSIRIS Team / MPS / UPD / LAM / IAA / RSSD / INTA / UPM / DASP / IDA (cb). **NASA:** (bc); SDO (br); JPL (clb). **4 NASA:** JPL-Caltech / MIT (cb); (crb, crb/Mars); JPL (fcrb). **4-5 NASA:** (cb). **5 NASA:** JHUAPL / SwRI (c); Johns Hopkins University Applied Physics (clb). **6 Corbis:** Nicholas Buer (bl). **6-7 NASA. 7 NASA:** JPL-Caltech (tc). **8-9 NASA:** SDO / Amari. **8 NASA:** AIA (clb). **9 Alamy Images:** WILDLIFE GmbH (crb). **NASA:** (cl, br). **10 NASA:** Goddard / Lunar Reconnaissance Orbiter (clb); Johns Hopkins University Applied Physics Laboratory / Carnegie Institution of Washington (cb). **Science Photo Library:** Dr. Ian Robson (br). **10-11 NASA:** Johns Hopkins University Applied Physics Laboratory / Carnegie Institution of Washington. **11 NASA:** JPL-Caltech / MIT (bc, crb/Jupiter); Johns Hopkins University Applied Physics Laboratory / Carnegie Institution of Washington (tr); JPL (cb); JPL-Caltech (cb/Mars). **12 ESA:** (c). **NASA:** (r, ca); JPL (cra). **13 Corbis:** Warren Faidley (ca). **Fotolia:** Strezhnev Pavel (cb). **NASA:** (l); James Yungel (bc). **14 NASA:** (tr). **14-15 Dreamstime.com:** Vibhision K Soni. **15 NASA:** (cr); JPL-Caltech / STScI / CXC / SAO (br). **16 NASA:** Goddard / Lunar Reconnaissance Orbiter; (bl, cra). **17 NASA:** (tl, cra); SDO (cl); Pat Rawlings (SAIC) (br). **18 Alamy Images:** Heritage Image Partnership Ltd (br); Sputnik (cr, bc); Michael Seleznev (fcr). **NASA:** (cl, bl). **19 Alamy Images:** SPUTNIK (tc). **Corbis:** Rykoff Collection (cra). **NASA:** (cla, clb, b). **21 NASA:** (cr). **22 NASA:** (tl, tr, br). **23 NASA:** (cb, bl, br). **24 NASA:** ESA (br). **24-25 NASA:** (all NASA). **26 NASA:** JPL-Caltech / University of Arizona (cl, c). **26-27 NASA:** JPL-Caltech. **27 NASA:** HiRISE, MRO,

LPL (U. Arizona) (crb); JPL-Caltech / Univ. of Arizona (bl). **28-29 NASA:** JPL-Caltech / MSSS (t). **28 Getty Images:** Photodisc / StockTrek (cl). **NASA:** ESA 2010 MPS for OSIRIS Team / MPS / UPD / LAM / IAA / RSSD / INTA / UPM / DASP / IDA (cla, cb); Pat Rawlings, SAIC (br); JPL / JHUAPL (cl/Asteroid 253 Mathilde); JPL-Caltech / UCLA / MPS / DLR / IDA (crb, fcl, bc, bl). **29 Getty Images:** Photodisc / StockTrek (bl). **NASA:** Goddard / Lunar Reconnaissance Orbiter (cb); JPL-Caltech / Univ. of Arizona (bc); JPL-Caltech / UCLA / MPS / DLR / IDA (br). **32-33 NASA:** JPL-Caltech / MIT (b/Jupiter). **33 NASA:** Johns Hopkins University Applied Physics Laboratory / Southwest Research Institute (cl); JPL-Caltech (tc); JPL (crb). **34 NASA:** JPL-Caltech / MIT (tl); Voyager Project, Calvin J. Hamilton (bl); ESA / K. Retherford / SWRI (br); JPL / DLR (cb); JPL (cl). **35 Corbis:** Jim Sugar (cra). **NASA:** JPL-Caltech / MIT (br); JPL / DLR (cr, cl, bc, br/Europa, fbr); JPL (bc/Lo). **36-37 NASA:** JPL / Space Science Institute. **36 NASA:** Caltech / Space Science Institute (tr). **37 NASA:** JPL (ca); JPL-Caltech / Space Science Institute (cr). **38 Alamy Images:** North Wind Picture Archives (crb). **NASA:** JPL-Caltech (t); NASA, ESA, and M. Showalter (SETI Institute) (bl). **39 NASA:** (t); JPL (clb); JPL / USGS (br). **40-41 NASA:** JHUAPL / SwRI. **40 NASA:** JHU APL / SwRI (crb, cra). **41 NASA:** (tc); JHUAPL / SwRI (c). **42 Alamy Images:** NG Images (tr). **NASA:** ESA, and M. Buie (Southwest Research Institute) (clb) Alan Stern as child courtesy of the Stern family. **43 NASA:** Bill Ingalls (tr); JHUAPL / SwRI (bl). **44-45 ESA:** Rosetta / NAVCAM (b). **44 ESA:** (cr). **NASA:** JPL Caltech / UCAL / MPS / DLR / IDA (cla, c, crb). **45 Alamy Images:** Galaxy Picture Library (cra); Stocktrek Images, Inc. (cla). **NASA:** (b, br). **Science Photo Library:** David Parker (cb). **49 NASA:** JHUAPL / SwRI (fcra). **50-51 NASA:** JPL / GSFC / SWRI / SSI (t); JPL-Caltech / Cornell Univ. / Arizona State Univ. (b). **50 NASA:** JPL-Caltech (clb). **51 Alamy Images:** M2 Photography (br). **Dreamstime.com:** Julien Tromeur (bc). **NASA:** JPL-Caltech / University of Arizona / University of Idaho (fcra). **52 NASA:** JPL-Caltech (ca); JPL (cr, br); NASA's Goddard Space Flight Center / NASA / JPL (clb). **53 NASA:** (bl, crb, tr); NASA Ames (ca). **54-55 NASA:** JPL. **55 Science Photo Library:** Detlev Van Ravenswaay (cra). **56

NASA:** ESA, and Z. Levay (STScI) (bl, c). **56-57 NASA:** ESA; G. Illingworth, D. Magee, and P. Oesch, University of California, Santa Cruz; R. Bouwens, Leiden University; and the HUDF09 Team (t). **57 NASA:** Ames / JPL-Caltech (bc). **58 NASA:** (br, fcl, cl, fcr); Johns Hopkins University Applied Physics (fclb); JPL-Caltech / MIT (cl/jupiter); JPL-Caltech (cr); JHUAPL / SwRI (fcra); Goddard / Lunar Reconnaissance Orbiter (cl/moon). **59 Alamy Images:** ITAR-TASS Photo Agency (bc). **Dorling Kindersley:** Royal Tyrrell Museum of Palaeontology, Alberta, Canada (ca). **NASA:** JPL-Caltech / UCAL / MPS / DLR / IDA (cl); SDO (tr); JPL (tl); Johns Hopkins University Applied Physics (crb). **60 NASA:** JPL-Caltech (bl). **61 NASA:** (tr, br)

Cover images: Front: Dorling Kindersley: Andy Crawford cra, NASA tr; Back: Corbis: Jim Sugar clb; ESA: tr; Spine: NASA

All other images © Dorling Kindersley
For further information see: www.dkimages.com

About the author

Sarah Cruddas is a space journalist and broadcaster with a background in astrophysics. She is frequently seen talking about space on British television, and appears on channels in the US such as National Geographic and Discovery Channel. Sarah specializes in space exploration and has reported on the subject from across the world. Her passion is to inspire the next generation of space explorers.